From Sand and Time

Poems

From Sand and Time

Poems

David Rose

A Vireo Book | Rare Bird

A Vireo Book | Rare Bird Books
453 South Spring Street, Suite 302
Los Angeles, CA 90013
rarebirdbooks.com

Set in Minion
Printed in the United States

10 9 8 7 6 5 4 3 2 1

Publisher's Cataloging-in-Publication data
Names: Rose, James David, author.
Title: From sand and time : poems / David Rose.
Description: First Trade Paperback Original Edition | A Genuine
Vireo Book | New York, NY; Los Angeles, CA: Rare Bird Books, 2017.
Identifiers: ISBN 9780997148640
Subjects: LCSH Poetry, American. | United States. Marine Corps—
Poetry. | Iraq War, 2003–2011—Poetry. | Marines—Poetry. | Post-
traumatic stress disorder—Poetry. | Afghan War, 2001—Poetry. |
BISAC POETRY / American / General
Classification: LCC PS3618.O78355 F76 2017 | DDC 813.6—dc23

With a brilliant philosophical mind and a seemingly endless font of creativity, this former Marine—and front-line warrior in the Global War on Terror—pours a lifetime of personal anguish, edge-of-civilization experience, and deep reflection into his collection of poems. Turn off all the noise and spend quiet, meaningful moments with Rose's work of art.

—**David Aretha**, editor, *World War II Chronicle* and *Nam: The Story of a Generation*

Visceral, heartbreaking, funny, introspective, and unflinchingly honest, the poetry of David Rose authentically captures the warrior experience.

—**Rich Ritter**, *Toil Under the Sun*

Author's Note

My generation: Just like every other that participated in an American war, the men and women who fought in the Global War on Terror are largely products of their environment.

Generation Y: Those who followed the Gen X'rs—born somewhere between the early eighties and early nineties... and driven to find purpose...or was it suffering from a lack of one? Referred to as Millennials—often pejorative and associated with things like consuming too much technology, or being self-obsessed. Whoever they were—we were—and whoever we are today, there is no denying we grew up in times as drastic as they were luxurious, as predictable as they could be foggy and perilous. Record-shattering divorce rates, the beginnings of the national opioid addiction—ever-dividing politics and a vast, foreign world suddenly made small by the push of a button. And in this whirlwind came those who donned the uniform. Among them the Marines—the owner of my early twenties and the central figure in this book.

Ask the most seasoned service member, or ask the most distant laymen, the veterans of the GWOT have been associated with two stereotypes—arguably at different poles on the spectrum of social understanding. On one hand, we are the invulnerable Boy Scouts who risked everything to spread democracy and protect our own. Shiny, golden figures—moral monoliths. On the other, sad creatures tormented by an unprecedented outbreak of PTSD.

The truth, as per usual, lies somewhere in between. The following poems will not support the Boy Scout caricature—just as much as they won't reinstate the stigmas of reluctance, being reactionary, or now being broken beyond all hope.

If we are to truly honor our vets, our wounded, and our war dead, than remembrance in its truest form is the highest species of honor. With that simple premise these pages were filled. The foul language, uncomfortable subject matter and the bouts of nihilism are not degradations to my generation of warfighter—and certainly not to the Marine Corps, which holds some of the fondest memories of my life—but rather a way to pay homage…in what is perhaps a unique language, our unique language, to and for a generation as complex and fierce as their wars, who proudly stepped up when called.

—David Rose, August 2017

Contents

BEFORE

Muddy

I've never trekked those islands,
I've never reached Saipan;
But the United States Marines,
They've gone there when they can!

Yeah, when the horn a blowin'
No more—some gave their all
Get red and wet and muddy
So red and wet and muddy
And I'd like to be lil muddy
While I hear the beck and call!

I've never seen muzzle fire,
Not one bang or scream or flame—
Birth men's loftiest summons,
And perhaps I'll fade in shame,

Unless I go get muddy
The glory and the maul—
So red and wet and muddy—
No, really wet and muddy
Must get red and wet and muddy
While I hear the beck and call!

The First God

He is the whole universe.
He is what they call God.
The day to night and night to day;
With a wink and a sought-after nod.

It was in the breeze, back on the old dirt road,
Where you taught me how to play;
So many sports and stick-fought war,
Long gone now is the day.

It was in the wood by your own father's home,
Where you showed me Man able to kill,
I cried for so many those fallen beasts,
You held me until I was still.

All was right,
In your sight,
Playing or toiling next to,
Rain or shine,
Growing divine,
In the shadow that stretched out from you.

He is the whole universe.
He was what they call God.
The day to night and night to day;
With a wink and a sought-after nod.

From your belly to chin I became,
Your many shirts ironed so white.
My world—the world—never the same,
When your toil became day and the night.

Mitts and bats turned to school boy's books,
One day we would certainly play,
And balls and bats to the web-covered nooks.
Then no more study and cometh the day:

A hard man like you would be so proud,
Into the uniform and into the gory.
No white shirts for me but the cannon so loud,
To me and mine shall go all the glory.

He was the whole universe.
He was what they call God.
The day to night and night to day;
With a wink and a sought-after nod.

Traded now the height of our stares,
Few too many, but that's nothing new,
Dad; the desk—Son; hammer pairs,
My sky the clearer the blue.

God became toiling mortal man,
As I s'pose all gods must go.
Forever long the day before change began,
As I s'pose all sons must know.

But in my own toiling sweat,
My nights and days are the same.
Perhaps forever in your debt,
If I live I'll carry the name.

In Need of a New Flame

Does all art come from sexual frustration?
Is sexual suppression the catalyst for artistic expression?
Can't stand looking at my tattoos sometimes,
Why'd I get so many?
To show off,
Appear hard,
Forge an identity?
I'm focusing my mind toward one goal.
Positive it will be just another let down.
Would love for once to be wrong;
Have that tiny, doubting, insecure monster shown things are
going to change.
Love for it exists in the way it wants it.

I live in my mind, picturing myself differently;
The mercenary,
The professor,
The rock star.
Never the introspective, sexually deprived Marine.

Need to gather the strength to step outside of fantasy,
Pursue the Now.
And it's scary as hell.

Dare to go against the grain with me.
Dare to thaw out a frozen mind.

I

I wish I had no family
I wish that I didn't have to put them through this
I try so hard not to give details of what I'm going to do
I can't help but reveal some of it though
I want to kill
I don't want any of my friends to die
I don't want to die
I want to go to Iraq though—so fucking bad
I wonder what kind of man I'll be if I live through this

We're all drunk and anticipating our end

I love her and she doesn't love me
I can't help this
I am not complaining
I don't know what I want anymore, except to kill
I think I'm the poster boy for the type of mindset they need
      over there
I am a fucking rockstar-murderer

There's no right end for this

I think about my death constantly
I think about my job constantly

Although my index finger is just flesh-n-bone, it's the most
      powerful thing the world has seen.
I want to be born in blood stained sand.

It Skips a Generation

You are my most beloved, sticks for guns high in the air,
Forts of cardboard sturdy, plastic six-guns the shining pair,
White headstones tall as you are—passing.
Your grandpa is over here.
Men who rubbed your head, close too,
Their faces forever clear.
We shall go look for hobgoblins—this cold nearby wood.
We shall feed all the duckies where I too young once stood.
We, yes, you and me, shall together beat back time's tiding,
If only for a moment before the warhorse comes riding.
Here is your stick—I brought it—here is your sword too,
And here is your coat to warm and guard,
Sky and baby-boy-eye blue.

The Lost Boys

Lost, lost, lost boys land in uniforms:
Trade in street gangs and C average student dorms.
For real now is that video game,
Time to do it—don't come home the same.

Squeaky clean and mighty mean,
The lost boys blossom—grand metal flower,
With fate a date once they graduate,
Ex-girlfriend's new boyfriends cower.

Oh only a few more yelled-at weeks,
Coming new illustrious peaks,
Climb them they will and more.
For someone told a listening few;
"Nothing you can't do,"
Bullies and dead-beat dads: settle the score.

Squeaky clean and mighty mean,
The lost boys hear the drum.
Long away the without-say day,
Glory be soon to come.

A Training Night with Gunny

Rain pouring,
A figure in black unknown to Man
Comes to touch with burning hand.
His existence is greatest, most prevalent when not exposed.
Comes to me when reality ends, imagination begins:
Exhaustion's throes.

Pep Talk Before the Range

Don't know or want to know about people's fucking minds.
My phone is getting smashed against a wall.
Ah yes, they must think I'm already over there.
BS, if I thought that I'd at least call and be sure.
Don't know why people don't give a fuck.
Can only write that I truly have grown to care so little,
My spite toward this species runs so fucking deep;
I dug right through the bottom.
I stand here now, secure, amped, feeling the mind question
    less and less.
There's nothing bad about me.
I'm okay.
Dished out money on their well-being,
Tried to listen to them in times of need,
Emulated that loyal friend I always wanted.
I have friends like that here,
But we're friends by an original obligation.
Survival.
We all know deep down when we're out we won't be the
    same.
Can't be the same friends.
This life is an adventure many times told,
The roads of; loneliness,
Doubt,
Confusion,
Sex,
Energy,
Vigor,

Spirituality conflicting and the quest for resolve.
Death is this ninety year monopoly game's get out of jail
   free card.
Obsessed with mortality and relish in eventual demise.
No wish to die, but no wish to live in denial.

Pre-deployment Leave

An orgasm brings suicide to mind.
How the two got mixed I'm not quite sure.
No one understands,
Especially me.
Can't stand a moment alone lately;
Go scurrying off to find something.
Goddamn.
Pathetic.
Realize how bad it is when I go home;
Parents end up crying,
Short fused with everyone,
Social skills so diminished.
I know a piece of me and he wants to die over there.
Not for the fantasy of a glorious funeral;
Fuck all that.
Just want all this to end sometimes.
Maybe a bullet is the only antidote for people like us.
More afraid of lifelong loneliness than an early death.
No one understands,
Hell—no one really understands anybody:
A bitter truth that sets one on a lonely path.
I stood there,
On the dock,
Family and friends,
Kids all around;
A good time;
A beautiful day.

Storm clouds headed toward me;

A black fist coming to grab.

Not us—me;

The foreshadowing of violence I'm about to undertake.

FIRST PUMP

First Letter From Home

I have given you life and name,
I have watched you battle with you,
From boy to man since your fire began,
Put thy hand to what few men do.

No up or down nor win or loss
Was mother gone prior this war,
Now gone is he who came out of me,
You on foreign dark shore.

I will carry the day and the hour
While you battle many men,
A country's care I do not bare,
True wars we both fight from within.

The Base

On the base there is no trace of joy or fun or mirth,
In the hours the mood so sours,
Men fight boredom all their worth.

The internet is down,
CO's a clown;
Came jibbering another jingle.
They swear one more so sullen day, this month of May,
The other side they'll go and mingle.

But not their lot, this traitor's dream,
Just a way to pass the time.
Not their lot, this traitor's dream,
Shoot at them an' they'll be fine.

On the base there is no trace of joy or fun or mirth,
In the hours the mood so sours,
Men regret their very birth.

Gunfire pops,
Sulking stops,
Go scrambling the magnificent men.
For now's the hour,
Great calling power,
Inflict on others times ten.

Hidden in dust,
The enemy must,
Be there—this they're sure.
But cracks and zips
Only crack whips
On horses familiar this tour.

On the base there is no trace of joy or fun or mirth,
"Where are they?!" the riflemen say,
Kicking and licking hard earth.

Not their lot, a traitor's dream,
Go scampering to the day,
Licking and kicking with their team,
This mirthless joyless May.

Then the CO announced,
And the riflemen pounced,
Internet; she be up an' runnin'.
Lows and highs;
When they can see enemy eyes,
Logged off they'll come out a gunnin'.

F O

How I wait for the blood-drawn hour,
Come Hell like rain an' steel like shower.

The Lady

Was walking out of our company area,
To my team's vehicle I went;
Burdened down by fatigue and gear,
Something covering my face.
Halfway through the no parking zone a middle-aged woman
 approached me.
Traditional all-black garb;
Emitting that eerie religious, mystical virtue.
Her face partly exposed,
Tattoos revealed themselves on her cheeks.
She was asking for directions.
I tried to explain I couldn't understand.
I tried to explain but whatever.
She motioned for me to unveil my face.
I did,
She did,
And it happened.
She shrieked,
Retracted,
A shrill noise and a storm of dark texture.
Somehow there was fear,
And a trust having been betrayed.
I woke up in the driver's seat of the Humvee,
We were in a patrol base digging up caches.

(O)CONUS

5/2 at 5:33 PM
Brother, brother o' mine
Hope you're doing well 'n' feelin' fine
Mom and Dad are still getting used
To the nightly news—pure utter abuse.
All the blown up Humvees,
The K I A,
The yellow star pleas,
To bring home you today.
Did I tell you our crazy neighbor just died?
Cussed out Dad and at Mom once had spied.
Yeah—stuffed in an ambulance, the way that they do,
Mom cried like crazy, think she was thinkin' of you.

5/3 at 1:04 AM
Tell Mom to cut out the damn waterworks,
Sis, this job has its sucks but it does have its perks.
Safer than yer loser boyfriend, that's just a fact,
Takin' that crazed highway, to his cute work 'n' back.
That's nuts the old codger's dead!
Dad put him on his ass once; two fists of pure swingin' lead.
You were too young, happened in our backyard,
Weirdo got froggy and Dad pulled his card.
Ha—makin' me miss you guys too much,
Be home soon—show ya pictures an' such.

5/3 at 12:21 PM
Ha Ha, He is not a man who loses!
Just 'nother path than you he chooses!
Not all are as tough-guy as you,
How's life over there? Give us a clue.
Oh, meant to tell ya—Kate 'n' Kerry divorced.
Kate's a wreck, Kerry cheated of course.

5/5 at 12:57 PM
Sorry for the little lag, dear gossipin' sis,
Had to work like a dog— now I'll reminisce;
About Kate and about Kerry and about that train wreck,
Ray Charles saw that one a comin', stacked against 'em the
    deck.
Can't talk much about life over here,
They monitor the emails, but you have nothing to fear.
I sleep and I work and I lift and I dream;
About seeing Ginny again, those blue eyes their gleam.

5/5 at 11:41 PM
God we partied all day,
Drunk as a skunk—spinnin' I lay.
Typing slow— do this message just right.
Speaking of Ginny—saw her tonight.
She misses you she says— proud yer defendin' our nation,
Just wishes—among other things—you'd see our graduation.
I wish so too—college in the fall.
By then you'll be with us, handsome and tall.

5/5 at 11:59 PM

I'll be there! Don't know about tall, but covered in snow,
Would write to ya lot more but, Sis, have to go…

Of Moe and Mo'

Yeah, Moe is Moe, and Mo' is Mo',
and never shall they change,
One fights to beat back crusaders,
one finds the country strange.

Mohammed preps his rifle now,
To kill the infidel.
He has slew many since coming here,
And sent them straight to Hell.
On one holy hit he took the dog tags,
Though dog tags he knows not the term,
Mo' wears them proudly around scarred wrist,
To outdo him their aerial-burn.
But a gun man is coming now,
Moe; from a farm near Bath, Maine.
Moe for country and red white and blue sir,
Moe the sworn enemy's bane.
"This spot is insanely hot,"
Moe's fire team lead justified,
"It was right here one week ago, yes,
"That three of ours suddenly died.
"There is where Smitty lost traumatic,
"His legs and that helmet impaled,
"Some haj gun man and bombs roadside,
"Thank God the big one failed.
"The ground is heavy with bombs roadside,
"But the walls hold things worse yet,
"Stash of liquor for the man who kills him,

47

"Range and scope his tools, this we won't forget.

"And his long range skill we don't forget,

"So enter homes at night,

"Kick in doors flip the chairs this our Higher's word,

"We'll see his heartbeat's blight.

"We'll have walls to our front and walls to our rear,

"And high hard walls above,

"We'll see no house goes unsearched now, him destroyed
    we'll be sure of."

The ready Maine boy fingered his gun,

A cold hard free black was it,

He'd fight for his land so free and so grand,

Once so now called so never quit.

The steady Maine boy fought the Muj here, so not fight
    them back home,

The land was odd and bare but always there,

Moe would work his black gun chrome.

So in this twilight no bombs roadside,

Moe kicks in the right door,

And finds Mo' asleep so still silent deep,

By the old long gun on the old floor.

And finds Mo' asleep so still silent deep,

But awoke rising face glowed,

Moe shot in his back with a loud crisp crack,

Just as the house explodes.

Ill aimed rounds from near camp had fell,

Moe saw dog tags 'round Mo's wrist,

But get to him never no way today,

Both laid in burned torn twist.

A warm young LT loaded both broke fighters,

One so GITMO bound,

Moe and Mo' lay in their blood stain beds,
Full fought for their own precious ground.

> *Yeah, Moe is Moe, and Mo' is Mo',*
> *and never shall they change,*
> *One fights to beat back crusaders,*
> *one finds the country strange.*

Klicks

Ten klicks 'til home and long began
This pageantry patrol;
Left seat right seat
No seat.
Miles marchin' took their toll.

But we not the ilk to squirm or squeam,
New guys will see the truth,
Nine klicks to home now—make 'er more
Fangs grown from long-gone tooth.

We marched near roads—known so well
Seasons spent ownin' this AO.
We must now impress,
They do so stress,
The relievers of our show.

Eight klicks to home and new guys sweat,
Passed the dogs a howlin'.
Now they wed,
But one month they shed,
Most gear that makes 'em growlin'.

Yeah—we heard a shiny one say,
"Complacent" at us poke.
But farm and berm have become our home,
Soon gone this ground our blood soak.

Seven klicks to base and the Sir is tall,
His equal so riding his shoulder.
A good long walk,
Armed stroll and a talk,
Same age but one so the older.

Give as a mortar, give us a shot,
Sneak and peak as you always will do.
Oil up these new boys,
Unsafety their toys,
And watch 'em battle out with so peakin' you.

Six klicks, five klicks, comin' up now on four,
A sip and a welcome high knee.
A farm and a berm—under our boots now,
Under our boots meets us klicks three.

Barrels up—the new ones gleam,
At the sight of a leather brown face.
Soon their aims will low,
And off we go,
To peel down longed cotton and lace.

Two klicks now and the minds a driftin',
Lace and such soft underneath,
But back to the warlands must yield,
No daydreamin' in field,
Lest one bullet be future's thief.

One klick 'til home and home it is,
Though mother would say it int' so,
Leave the best,
Join the rest,
And my how the medals will glow.

BETWEEN

East Meets West

"How was that drill instructor; Thomas Cruise,"
Said the Island born Marine.
"Top Gun—ha, hills that would make-ya glad you choose,
Mosquito Island; sweat and steam."

San Diego Marine gloated,
That California hill-won mirth,
"And don't forget our coyotes—
Rat fuckin' for all their worth."

"You warm-weathered Holly Woods,"
Laughed a man made in the swamp,
"Ours is one of long proud history,
Yours is flash and sun and pomp."

"Get the hell outta here,
You been to MCR—hill-humpin'—D?
Lifers yell, horseshoes a shinin',
Same for you as was same for me."

"I'll shake your Holly hand next time,"
Said Marine made from Island grounds.
"But for now let's sit at a bar top here,
On me; first of many rounds."

Dry Barracks

Dry barracks the dry barracks
Cuz our CO wants an award
Too many damn demerits
From his riflin' triflin' horde.

In to a month-dry barracks
March the drinkin' stinkin' men
Beg your pardon—out in town
Be seein' ya now an then.

On to base we be a swervin'
Cuz the barracks be a dry
Hate to be that PFC
Who puts MPs on bloomin' high.

Dry barracks the dry barracks
CO'll be stuck at silver leaf
Crashes call—one an all
From HM3 to Chief.

Short Entry, Gents

They wanna know what it's like,
I would too if I had never experienced it.
Truth is it scares me how not a big deal it really is.
Nothing changes.
Still have a problem walking past people and what to do with
 my eyes.
Thought a firefight would change all that.

A Night in the Barracks with Jim Morrison

Poetry says nothing
It merely opens doors
Choose the one you like

Will you love me tonight?
I never truly know why I write
I see flames
Glass broken in the falling rain
Spilling onto a darkened earth
Black but not dirty in the silence
Let go of it
Whatever it is
Standing, or should I say suspended?
Dancing in twilight
A mere figment
Is that all?
Will you love me tonight?

Tonight's the only one that ever matters
Cuz here we are.

The Virtuous

Swanson yelled out, veins out the neck,
Then Crotty swelled with mirth,
Weary sharp eyes blinking, bones tested lock,
Between the heavens and earth.

And Swanson said, from eager chest,
"I have come under heaven's right
To offer you the Old Breed virtue now
And be the fight in the fight.

"I can give you clean faces, true and proud
And deeds right out of the Book."
But Crotty smirked gleamed glared and then spit
Knowing the stomped mean boots the earth shook.

And they then fast passed Swanson's eyes
Gun-holding virtuous man,
Hard faces dirty, cursers galore,
Howling from where it all began.

"Praise spit and Hellfire," Crotty crowed,
"Spit and Hellfire battles won
You're virtue take on a different shade
When battling is to be done."

'Where is this true virtue then," Swanson said,
"For your medals are many

Is it in the proud hallow bugle call
There anywhere if any?"

"I see march and dig," Crotty said,
"The whole world is you're field of fire,
But I can see them marching still
And march hard with them 'til we tire;

"And this virtue goes where they're marching,
When gone no more the warrior call;
I see this virtue you so youngly speak
Exalted, the drunken brawl.

"Honor is a life's morning sky unbroken
Trinkets and foibles wiped clean;
And one has seen on bloody fields hard fought
Triumphant virtuous mean,

"Which gives the latter skies their reveal
And men their earned seasoned face,
While bugle calls come and go day and night
The virtuous men embrace."

Ghost

Please want me to be a part of your life
I can't make you love me.
You are the only thing in this dismal world that makes me
        cling to reality
In that you are the only thing that makes me want to be real.
Real to the millions of unaware,
The people who the aware *defend*.

I say please in desperation.
I am desperate, you know?
Somehow I seem to mask my drowning being to everyone
Played off as weird—eccentric.
I promise you, it's not:
I wake up sometimes not knowing where I am
I fall asleep sometimes very scared.

When I'm driving all I do is stare at everyone and wonder
        what their problem is.
Maybe I'm the problem.
I go to all the old haunts of my youth,
And they are exactly that—haunted.
Not a soul in this world occupies the places I once held dear.

I have the ability to see life as a wondrous motion,
A living art.
There are eternities in a moment,

I see such beauty in things so that I can't even describe them
in words.

Words are third rate to what I see and feel.

I am so sad sometimes that suicide isn't even an option.

I believe suicide brings damnation.

Damnation means you still exist,

Just damned.

Still the same jungle.

Sometimes I want to unravel the fabric of existence and just
not be;

Have everything just not be anymore.

Disappointment is the stamp on the soul,

The motto of the life of a ghost.

Most of the time I don't know what I am;

Strong.

Weak.

Successful.

A loss.

I do know that I am one fucked up motherfucker.

Anyone who says they know me and disagrees is either
refusing to see or too naive.

Billions of red flags.

Because I have realized that my ability to see and feel lives
within this one, and to touch the very essence of things so
magnificent in both their cruelty and their majesty is a solo
act. This has birthed the reality that the life I view from these
eyes isn't and never will be the life that others see. Some may
say it is a gift to see everything so grand. But what is beauty if
you can't share it with the greatest beauty of all?

I am coming to believe that my being of constant war is a
being incapable of receiving love in that respect. The respect
of a woman who admires and cherishes you, a woman
that—ah, fuck it.

There need not be such a needed sorrow for a ghost.
When he dies his remembrance means nothing.
No one remembers him.
Only what they thought he to be.
No one could venture forth into the abscess of his core.
And why the hell should they?

I ask now two requests:
Please allow me to mean the second, and
Forget you knew me.
It's like seeing a rusty piece of farm equipment in the middle
    of an abandoned field.
It may be there, but it really isn't,
Its existence died with its use.

Might Be Going To Quantico

Recon has taught me something invaluable;
I am not an island.
People need people,
I am the most reluctant introvert on earth to admit it.
During the desired-island age,
Or at least to be the man on the isle,
I wasn't.
Rather I was a peninsula,
The man on the peninsula;
Back turned to the mainland,
Only seeing the sea at all sides.
The finger of land barren,
Scorched by fires.
Some brought by nature,
Others by my own devices.
The man standing on the wasteland,
Ignoring the lush main.
Why?
Fear of the unknown.
Hate for the known.
Never dared to imagine how much strength it takes to be so
    vulnerable.
Already knew how much strength it took to do the rest.

One Pump an' Done

Yeeeaahhhhh—on tarmac again,
Thisssssssssss—the last one my friend.
Half year more,
Through that door,
Grand paycheck I will carry,
A beard will grow,
And back to snow,
And with you-know-who I'll marry.

SECOND PUMP

Human Aggression

It's much like a whirlwind hot,
Hot whirlwind live in me.
Some sort of violation here,
So plain for all to see.
Change from man into beast I go,
Instead the hangman's tree.

Or shoot or pierce or bash; my end;
Not I—the reaper's possession.
White heat burgeoning in the flesh,
Prolong thy mortal obsession.
And by this one thing yet still I so live;
This whirlwind of human aggression.

Armored Smile

Kicked back in the breeze,
That warm summer's ease,
Win and slay and ensure it;
Armored youth, sharp mind as sharp tooth,
Lounging in comfortable turret.

Mark this day,
So joyous and gay;
Here in the summer's feast.
For gorge on the war,
Men by the score;
The marvelous high-headed beast.

Calm in the din;
Dozen infantry men,
March as dance, sing as play,
Smiles begot,
No aching or rot,
This marvelous victorious day.

Eyes Shutting

I try to live my entire life, to
Not fear flame as I lay dying.

The Crazed Young Hardened Boy

"Because I'm made for bloody war
I'm not made for the grief,"
Spoke that crazed young hardened boy
Who fights with own belief,
"Not to croak in an old folk's home,
Not knowing who I am,
That is all I demand, Chaps,
From your good-book's all-knowing lamb."

"Caring are your words, Chaplain,
Don't let me cause silence,
Keep up this quaint din, Chaplain,
Tell me the good in violence.
But know I have what few boys do
Marrow made for the fray,
I have love for the gun's bark and fire,
Don't armed lost souls win the day?"

The chaplain saw the crazed young boy
Called to war like David of old,
"Made," he said "You here sustain,
And that I also hold,
Born war fighter you are not alone
The past holds boys so same,
Sword and shield, maybe talked like you
Some forgot—some with fame.

Hot blood rage can be a tool
Wield it righteously or ill,
Source of all good beckons
Some capable to kill;
Hateful heart dwell in miseries
War boy though you hate-filled seem,
Tasks set on human heart hard
Yet those of you still beam."

"You might be right, Chap-a-lain,
I hear what you preach me,
Alas though, I don't coddle fate
Let's agree to disagree.
Clever: 'look and you shall find'
Makes any quest fit your book,
Whether righteous whether godless
Is still God's pawn and rook.

"I'll stay my course, Chap-a-lain,
And I'm sure you'll stay yours too
Brain blood bone and suffering;
What I want to do.
God's work my work our work,
We'd sit and ponder more,
But yours truly loves gun barking,
For me it is no chore."

Lady Luck

Bryan:
Always wanted to feel that great big boom;
The thunderously mortar from yon horizon!
We fled so fast,
But it didn't last;
Roll another die to be cast,
The torturous, calamity—not our doom.
Just unlucky man this day dies in.

Ryan:
My senses must be a true wreck after that,
These words are sophomoric at greatest.
We could have died.
News flash—yer recruiter lied,
Not made of stone, no god on our side,
Empty are errands where we are stuck at,
"Great big boom"; just the latest.

Bryan:
Is there no pulse in you, Brother-in-arms?
No hot blood in those once-throbbing veins?
Alive and here,
You and I, brother dear,
How can a life be without fear?
And Ryan remember; luck hung her charms
On you and I—mountain or plains.

Ryan:
So depend on fortune good say you,
I left my new wife and our daughter;
To run amuck,
Under punitive ruck,
Regards; that fickle bitch called Luck.
Geisler and Gunny Paul; out of her view;
Bored stiff then lambs for the slaughter.

Bryan:
Grief me, you—only together this moment do we make,
Pull me back down to sullen earth.
Heavy my kit,
Must now admit,
How much I so-of'n hate this shit?
Happily asleep? Well now I awake,
Go we to find our dismal worth?

Ryan:
Come on—let's talk no more this sorrow.
There goes it; our punishing sun;
Yonder the farther crest,
Half-klick to the rest,
With them you can laugh in madman's jest;
All these breaths we do but borrow,
And I'll lone count the moment 'til we're done.

The Westys

Jill Westy left her husband
Captain in his corps.
She went back home to Phoenix
Her parent's held-open door.
Jill Westy left her husband
That way put her on the floor.

Jill Westy left her husband
First love; his career.
Just liquor for his lady
His body never near.
The desert was his dwelling
And it scorched her toe to ear.

Jim Westy went to Mosul
Time and time again.
His office of two-by-sixes
Held toil, sweat, and friend.
Jim Westy went to Mosul
His marriage not to mend.

Jim Westy stood in Mosul
Lone rocket aimed.
Brother's sad tired body
On two-by-sixes maimed.
Here now Captain Westy wipe clean
Mind and body and proclaimed:

"My life my wife my sorrow,
So dreadfully intertwine,
I have given so much for others
Now I give to what is mine."
Flagged-coffin flew out at one
And with it Westy arrived at nine.

Jill Westy flew from Phoenix
Jim Westy from God knows where.
Base's golden morning
Green and familiar fair.

THEREAFTER

The Bird Daydreams of Being a T-rex Again

It's those times when you don't feel your best,
It's those times where you feel that if you opened up,
Even the slightest,
You'd be invaded.
Defiled.
It's those times where you feel like you can be crushed.
It's those times,
It's those,
Well, it's just those times.

Poetry is so silly,
It's at its worst when it rhymes.
Poets muddy the shallow waters around them to make them
seem deep.

Hindsight is clear as hell,
Or so I suppose.
Coming back to this place is a strange thing.
Nobody is going to see eye to eye with you now.
I predicted leaving them was going to be hard.
It's so strange,
How they are so calm and cool.
Not me.

I sure learned one thing;
My time in Lejeune is outdated and over.
It was a good thing;

Finding out for myself.
No big deal.

Last night he was talking about how one of our dead is in
     Hell.
I couldn't help but feel real creeped out by the whole thing.
Morbid.
Tasteless.
But humor none the less.
I wondered—who was the strong one;
The mourner or the jester?—
As I pictured a mangled, burning corpse,
Crawling over me,
Whispering in my ear to shut up the joke-teller.

The guys getting out do not realize what's waiting for them.
Doesn't make me any better,
Just a guy who got out before they did.
In a small way a sad thing;
Times wanting only to be an operator again.
The job.
A team.
The bird daydreams of being a T-rex again.
Didn't try to convince them,
They'll find out on their own.
Moving,
Moving,
Moved the fuck on.

Once again,
A foot print.

Left on soil but never seen,
Go back—it's gone.
A lot of things in perspective.
Now I am officially out of the Marines.

Gonna Take Away Our Guns

Bipolar is this 'Merican brain
Flag wavin' and armed to the teeth
Praise those in service but martial law will come
What paranoia that lay underneath

The man and boy and woman and girl
Thanking us but with watchful eye
That one day on them we'll so easily turn
With a door knock all freedom will die.

And with such death we take way the gun
From man, boy, woman, and girl
Modern day patriot run wild backwood
While enslaving plan high above shall unfurl

But staunch uniforms know no such day
Just day ranges and the GI Bill
Sully our worth and our heart and our name
For idle minds to feed such cheap thrill

Come the day—those UN ships
Come yonder the Gulf or Atlantic
Uniformed man, boy, woman, and girl
Stand with ya—the invaders be frantic.

Lower your guard, raise your flag
No uniform be after your arms
Go back to your office, your mud mixin', your truck,
Enjoy those big well-guarded farms.

It's Been a Year

A crumbling city far away,
Souls wander a far street go.
There I walked, and where we once there talked,
Of things which living men know.

Did they tell you my city is gone?
In it I walk same as you.
Search for the place which held our bright grace,
Together; what living men knew.

Digi-Desert Straitjacket Man

The war having long been over for me—
Thrust back into it—
Another comrade dies overseas.
Ripped out of the pallid Now;
Mind racing,
When was the last time I saw him?
A rented suit and a flight later…

Digi-Desert Straitjacket Man
Thrust back into the warfighting land

Fight and see a friend die
Fight through the aggressive beggars and the morbidly
    obese to later see his wreathed grave.
The oft-sensationalized and cliche question;
"What the hell did we fight for?"
Needles the mind of anyone who has stared down at
    familiar names on Arlington headstones.
Standing next to the rough, often imitated, men of my ilk;
Some in dress uniforms,
Others not.
Men from my old unit who retired during my time as a
    gunslinger,
Now bearded and a bit gray;
Orbiting the military,
Forever seeking the grand purpose of some irrecoverable
    deployment.

A kid squirming in a tiny black suit,
Born when his dad and I were in Karma.
A Staff Sergeant I knew,
Now a Sergeant Major.
The ritual over, thus the descent back into…it.

Digi-Desert Straitjacket Man
Jumps in an out of the great frying pan

The gnarled mouth opens.
Jagged canines burst upward and tower:
Congested marquees for fast-food feedlots.
Another abscessed fang;
A gas station attracting the rising flotsam.
And then…
Looming over all else,
The fetid molar:
Walmart.
Back to the towns, jobs, and the normal life.

Digi-Desert Straitjacket Man
Contemplates his condition whenever he can

Days later;
After the traffic jams and an insurance salesmen passes me
        in toe-shoes and an "Infidel" T-shirt
I know why my dead friend had fought—
Why I fought.
During the bloodshed I believed the hardships would begat
        some glorious, glorious existence,
But what I could never name.

Was I to find happiness and peace returning as a warrior to
    the tradition;
Stability,
Security,
Comfort?
Sounds easy enough—
Until you realize all your heroes died of heroin, the bullet, or
    the bottle.
Then,
After enough of Americana's wry grimace,
Creeping Jesus,
It hits me:
We carved our own unique corner of reality,
In real time,
Untouchable by the covetous outsider-mass.
The bland and proper fixtures of our parent-society were
    never the goal.
Nothing
No citizenry at home,
Nor collapse of the shithole ground we once occupied,
Can diminish the brotherhoods we arc-welded,
Done so with the rifle.
A week later,
Standing in the kitchen on a tight-fist February morning,
"A real man isn't afraid to show his feelings" she says.
I think of the men who were willing to die for me;
And she's right,
A real man, in fact, isn't afraid to show his feelings.
But there aren't tears being hidden,
No thunderous fit pressed up behind puckered lips and
    locked teeth.

There really is nothing there.
Well there is something,
But showing certain feelings through actions makes you a
    hero in one land,
A murderer in another.

Digi-Desert Straitjacket Man
The laughable inversion of PTSD—the indelicate flower
Digi-Desert Straitjacket Man
Make my heart beat hard once more—maybe an RPG to
liven the lunch hour.

A Vet Writer Nickerson

The stuck vet writer Nickerson
Was angry tired and bored;
All he could write, type, say, or post,
Were demands of howling horde.

As he scribbled in his pad,
Night had befell and grew,
Yet again the mob pled and cried,
And he wished for something new.

"There is no thirst for my real voice,
"For Veteran means just War,
"My hero wrote of many things
"But myself just flags and gore."

He wept a dry, ghost vet'ren weep
Away now pen and pads;
His own hero lived life and art,
Not failure like their dads.

Sleep overtook, coming many dreams,
His mind bleak as blackest moor;
His bed wrestled him 'round and 'round,
His hero's words adore.

Upon the day the email-blast
Night burned back fierce and hot,
The trapped vet writer Nickerson
Would rather be than not.

"Artist's Dark Age! My luck is nil
"To be born in this time,
"I'd make too, he once penned many things:
"Bliss. Loss. Life. Freedom. Rhyme."

He did now as he ever did,
Long message bit by bit;
Yet 'nother limp work feedback more:
"Brother, you so killed it!"

But then came soon a known held name,
"… your words are a lot like him."
The glued vet writer Nickerson
Went numb from limb to limb.

"Did you know that," the *bro* wrote;
"He hated his own voice?"
The stuck vet writer Nickerson
He chewed on his own choice.

"Thank God for men like you and he,
"Keep your words coming, bro!
"You could write plays and novels, but
We'd hate to see you go."

He picked up his pen—mighty it,
With ideas flowing from the heart,
Life often gives what one may know
In impact as in art.

Drink Up

Our branch has battled so many bold men,
The Deutsch and the Jap and the Cong.
Mean sons of mean bitches 'vry now and again,
But every one of them worthy of song.
Yet no great foe for Gen'ration Y,
Boy beaters, girl slavers galore,
Respect for Grandad's but not for my,
Sons of the sand loath and abhor.

So drink up honored Grampa Joe,
Fought those wily Germans;
Those big blonde hardened fightin' men
Steadfast and so determined.
Go fly and see those so few left,
Bent now; old and gray,
For father and the fatherland,
So similar shared the day.

We fought ours in their sprawlin' desert,
We fought 'em on hills of dust,
We would have fought 'em to our last good measure,
If good measure'd been asked of us.
But alas we had no big blonde men,
No German to equal us great.
We only had the sons of sand,
So unworthy such twist of fate.

So drink up grinnin' Grampa Joe,
Vet'ren of the Chosin;
Those little yellow fightin' men
With you just as frozen.
Go fly and see those may be left,
Good officers to blame,
For both your nostalgic miseries,
Now just as then so same.

We fought ours on a mountain,
We fought ours through fire's flame,
We drank from the reaper's fountain,
But goddamn—just ain't the same.

So drink up smilin' Uncle Joe,
Steamy jungle's dead of night;
Those little yellow sneakin' men
At ya comin' to pick a fight.
Go fly and see those many left,
From farm to war then back,
Toil in steam as you both once did,
Burdened life-giving pack.

The papers claim to know the aim
Of these cowards and misguided fools.
But it's the few who came into the barren game
That know—foreign policy's tools.
And if there are left a million doors to kick,
We'll be kicking 'til our last heartbeat.
Able and willing and god-awful quick,
But fate—know we call you a cheat.

And They Said I'd Beat Her in My Sleep

This stranger.

Moon wanes over such sleek body seen.
Time away robs and instills.
Eyes that held mountains once so familiar,
Now shows these bleak foreign hills.

When she returns from the voyage I made,
Hope she dancing amidst life-giving flame,
Not of steel, but of silk and of mirth.
And I hope I can be just the same.

It's Been Ten Years

Best day, best days,
Go both ways,
Behind us and wait yonder shore.
Such gold morning met us back then,
But by God we can hope there's still more.

VA Form 21P-530

I have rode the red high mountains,
I have plumbed the depths with ease,
Burning and gone and up before dawn,
The able young man overseas.

Were there ever a feat I not bested,
When able and cunning and keen,
Before time as a thief—'fore age, tear, an' grief,
When things lost were readily seen?

I have withered the way we must wither,
Medals for far off the day,
Glory my flower—cometh the hour;
Content my head when where it shall lay.

Must get red and wet and muddy
While I hear the beck and call!